Original title:
The Chill of the Woods

Copyright © 2024 Swan Charm
All rights reserved.

Author: Sara Säde
ISBN HARDBACK: 978-9908-1-1366-1
ISBN PAPERBACK: 978-9908-1-1367-8
ISBN EBOOK: 978-9908-1-1368-5

The Stillness After First Snowfall

The world is draped in white,
Hushed whispers fill the air.
Children laugh, pure delight,
Snowflakes dance without a care.

Footprints mark the path anew,
Joyful shouts, hearts entwined.
Crisp and bright, the sky so blue,
In this stillness, peace we find.

Icicles glimmer in the sun,
Nature's beauty, fresh and bright.
Gathered close, we all become
Part of winter's pure delight.

Hot cocoa warms our hands,
Storytellers gather 'round.
In the calm, unity stands,
Festive echoes all around.

Emotions Woven in Thistledown

Breezes dance with gentle grace,
Thistledown whirls in twilight.
Every heart finds its safe space,
Woven dreams take flight tonight.

Laughter echoes in the glen,
Hopeful wishes softly soar.
Friends return to laugh again,
Embraces shared forevermore.

Under stars that brightly gleam,
Whispers of the heart are shared.
Life unfolds like a sweet dream,
Each moment held, cherished, bared.

Beneath the moon's watchful glow,
Gatherings warm our spirit's core.
In the soft light, feelings grow,
Thistledown binds us, evermore.

Luminous Night in a Leafy Sanctuary

Moonlight dances on the leaves,
Crickets sing their evening song.
In the night, each heart believes,
In this haven, we belong.

Fireflies twinkle, stars take flight,
Nature's pulse, a gentle beat.
Gathered here, in shared delight,
Our laughter makes the night complete.

Branches sway with softest grace,
Echoes of our joy resound.
In this magical, sacred space,
Friendship blooms all around.

Pine-scented breezes kiss our cheeks,
Memories woven, heart to heart.
In the night, our spirit speaks,
A festive bond, we'll never part.

Chirps and Whispers of a Winter's Night

The night wraps all in silence,
Whispers of the snowflakes fall.
Crickets chirp with sweet defiance,
Winter's magic, a warm call.

Around the fire, stories spin,
Voices rise like sparks to sky.
In this circle, love begins,
Joyful moments drift on high.

Timid stars begin to peek,
Shimmering through branches bare.
In the calm, our hearts all speak,
Festive warmth fills chilly air.

As we share our hopes and dreams,
Embers glow, a vibrant dance.
Winter's night, or so it seems,
Ignites our hearts in joyful trance.

Shiver of the Forest Floor

In the glade, laughter rings clear,
Sparkling lights twinkle near.
Footsteps dance on a carpet of gold,
Warming hearts from the winter's cold.

Carols echo through the trees,
A festive spirit carried on the breeze.
Children's joy, a bright display,
Celebrating life in a vibrant way.

Breath of the Winter Grove

Snowflakes waltz upon the air,
Each flake whispers, none compare.
Glistening branches hold the night,
Embracing warmth in soft moonlight.

Gathered round the crackling fire,
Stories shared, hearts grow higher.
The scent of pine, sweet and pure,
Festive moments that endure.

Ghosts in the Timberland

Whispers linger in the mist,
Old tales told, we can't resist.
Lanterns sway, casting shadows bold,
Celebrations rich, stories unfold.

Charmed by visions, we embrace,
Memories dance, a warm embrace.
In every branch, in every beam,
Timberland glows with a dream.

Frostbitten Leaves

Leaves of copper, shimmer white,
Beneath the stars, a wondrous sight.
Joyful hearts filled with mirth,
As frost adorns this hallowed earth.

Feast and laughter fill the air,
Echoes of love, everywhere.
Around us glows a magical hue,
In the festive night, all feels new.

In the Embrace of Autumn's Breath

The trees don coats of gold and red,
Leaves dance lightly, a warm breeze led.
Pumpkins bright in fields they gleam,
Harvest songs weave joy's sweet dream.

Bonfires crackle 'neath a starlit sky,
Children laugh and let their kites fly.
Spiced cider warms in hands held tight,
Autumn whispers joy, a pure delight.

Silent Echoes Among the Trees

Whispers in the woods as daylight fades,
Rustling branches, nature's soft masquerades.
Beneath the boughs, a symphony stirs,
Echoing laughter, as each memory blurs.

Golden hues adorn the winding paths,
Frolicking creatures share their joyous laughs.
Crickets serenade the moon's gentle rise,
In silence they dance beneath starry skies.

Midnight's Embrace in the Thicket

The night is alive with glimmers and sighs,
Lanterns flicker like stars in the skies.
Floral scents mingle, inviting the night,
Under the moon, everything feels right.

Rustling whispers as shadows unfold,
Stories exchanged in a bond made bold.
With hearts in rhythm and spirits so free,
Midnight's embrace, pure ecstasy.

Frost-Kissed Leaves Underfoot

A crystal layer drapes the ground,
Each step crunches, a joyful sound.
Breezes carry laughter from afar,
As we gather 'neath the twinkling stars.

Cocoa warms our hands as we share,
Frosted whispers bubble in the air.
The world aglow, in festive cheer,
Winter's magic—every heart draws near.

Breath of Winter Through the Branches

A whispering chill in the frosty air,
Laughter echoes with a vibrant flair.
Snowflakes twirl in a waltzing breeze,
Nature's joy wraps around like trees.

Colors sparkle in a snowy spree,
Harmony sings, setting spirits free.
The world adorned in shimmering white,
A festive dance beneath moonlight bright.

Lament of the Withering Ferns

Once so vibrant in emerald hue,
Now they sway with a wistful view.
Each frond wilts in the fading glow,
Yet memories linger of times aglow.

The dance of autumn whispers goodbye,
As falling leaves in the breeze sigh.
Still, they share tales of days so grand,
In the heart of the forest, a timeless band.

The Hushed Solitude of the Glade

Silent echoes in the tranquil wood,
Where solitude wraps like a sweet hood.
Sunbeams waltz through the leafy lace,
In each shadow, a warm embrace.

Whispers of nature, soft and low,
Inviting all with a gentle flow.
Here, festivities in silence bloom,
A joyous peace within the gloom.

Lament of the Withering Ferns

Once so vibrant in emerald hue,
Now they sway with a wistful view.
Each frond wilts in the fading glow,
Yet memories linger of times aglow.

The dance of autumn whispers goodbye,
As falling leaves in the breeze sigh.
Still, they share tales of days so grand,
In the heart of the forest, a timeless band.

The Hushed Solitude of the Glade

Silent echoes in the tranquil wood,
Where solitude wraps like a sweet hood.
Sunbeams waltz through the leafy lace,
In each shadow, a warm embrace.

Whispers of nature, soft and low,
Inviting all with a gentle flow.
Here, festivities in silence bloom,
A joyous peace within the gloom.

Ghostly Dances of the Silver Birch

White bark glistens in the evening light,
Dancing shadows take joyous flight.
A vision trails where the moonbeams blend,
In the silver glade where dreams transcend.

Whirling spirits in a woodland trance,
Each flicker invites a dreamlike chance.
Joyful whispers through branches weave,
In silver tones, we believe and achieve.

Echo Chamber of Harsh Whispers

In the chaos, laughter rings,
Voices rise like joyful flings.
Amidst the clamor, spirits soar,
Hearts entwined, we crave for more.

Colors burst, a vivid show,
With every step, new faces flow.
Echoes bounce off distant walls,
Together we embrace the calls.

Treading Softly through the Whispering Pines

Beneath the boughs, the sunlight plays,
Dancing lightly through leafy maze.
Whispers swirl in the crisp, cool air,
Nature's hymn, a soothing prayer.

Laughter twirls like autumn leaves,
Joyful hearts that the forest weaves.
In this haven, sweet and bright,
We wander on, pure delight.

Shadows of Echoing Silence

In twilight's glow where silence dwells,
Magic lingers, our hearts it compels.
Stars awaken, a shimmering throng,
In stillness, we hum a silent song.

Dreams take flight on gentle wings,
Whispers of fate as the night sings.
Together in this sacred space,
We find our joy, our peaceful grace.

Veils of Crystal Among the Green

Through emerald leaves, the sunlight streams,
Dewdrops dance like tangled dreams.
Nature's jewels, each sparkle bright,
We gather 'round in pure delight.

With every breath, the world is new,
In quiet moments, friendships brew,
Laughter and joy, a vibrant seam,
Life woven in a festive dream.

An Evening's Shroud in the Woods

The sun dips low, the shadows play,
A golden glow meets twilight's sway.
Laughter dances on the breeze,
Whispers of joy among the trees.

Fireflies flicker, a twinkling show,
Nature's lanterns in the afterglow.
Friends gather round in warmth and cheer,
An evening's charm, so bright and clear.

Songs of old fill the night air,
With voices joined in love and care.
The scent of pine and crisp, cool air,
A festive heart, a moment rare.

The stars awaken, a silver lace,
Each spark a wish in this sacred space.
Together we share this wondrous night,
In the woods, our spirits take flight.

Unraveled Threads of Nature's Song

In the meadow blooms a vibrant hue,
Each petal whispers, soft and true.
Children frolic, laughter so sweet,
Nature's song beneath our feet.

Glistening dew on the blades of grass,
Moments cherished, too quick to pass.
With every step, joy's melody,
In harmony with the bumblebee.

Banners of color, the trees adorned,
Songs of birds celebrate dawn's morn.
A tapestry woven with wondrous threads,
Together we dance, where magic spreads.

As the sun bows low and shadows blend,
This knitted joy, it has no end.
In each heart lives a festive cheer,
Unraveled love that draws us near.

A Symphony of Fallen Memories

Leaves twirl in the autumn air,
Laughter echoes, a joyful flare.
Colors dance beneath the trees,
Whispers float upon the breeze.

Crisp cider warms the evening glow,
As fireflies put on their show.
Friends gather 'round with cheer in sight,
Weaving tales under twinkling light.

Every smile, a fleeting glance,
In this moment, hearts will dance.
Memories linger, laughter's song,
In the fest of life, we all belong.

Glistening Veil of the Morning Mist

Dewdrops sparkle on blades of grass,
A gentle hush as moments pass.
Golden rays peek through the veil,
Nature's whispers, sweet and frail.

Birds sing a melody so bright,
Welcoming dawn, a wondrous sight.
Colors bloom, the world awakes,
Joyous laughter as daylight breaks.

In the mist, dreams come alive,
Hearts rejoice, and spirits strive.
Every breath, a promise made,
In this embrace, our fears will fade.

Moonlit Pathways Through the Undergrowth

Silver beams kiss the forest floor,
Guiding steps to discover more.
Crickets chirp their nightly tune,
While stars twinkle like fond balloons.

Together we dance in shadowed light,
Lost in magic, pure delight.
Shapes and forms weave a tale,
Underneath the moon's soft veil.

Adventurers in the night so clear,
With hearts ablaze, we conquer fear.
Every path a mystery to unfold,
In this journey, brave and bold.

Secrets Found in an Icy Grove

Snowflakes twirl like whispers sweet,
Beneath the trees, we softly meet.
Frosted branches glisten bright,
In this serene, enchanting night.

Laughter dances through the frost,
In this wonderland, never lost.
Every secret, a tale to share,
Embraced by winter's cold, fresh air.

Candles flicker in the hush,
As hearts awaken in the rush.
Together, we find warmth and cheer,
In icy realms, love draws us near.

A Tapestry of Frosted Twilight

Twinkling lights in the evening air,
The laughter of friends, we gather near.
With mugs of warmth, we share delight,
As snowflakes dance in the soft moonlight.

A tapestry woven in shimmering threads,
With whispers of joy, our spirits spread.
Each moment cherished, forever bright,
Wrapped in the glow of this frosted night.

The Quiet of the Year's End

The clock strikes twelve, a moment to pause,
Reflecting on the year with gentle applause.
Candles flicker, shadows play,
Memories echo as the hours sway.

In the quiet hush of a winter's embrace,
We find the magic in this sacred space.
With wishes whispered, hearts take flight,
Celebrating the peace of this starry night.

Whispers of Frosted Pines

Amidst the pines, a soft wind sings,
A symphony of joy that nature brings.
Beneath the branches, the snowflakes gleam,
In a world transformed, we chase the dream.

Frosted whispers through the woodland glide,
With every breath, warmth fills inside.
Together we gather, our spirits entwined,
In the heart of winter, love is defined.

Shadows Beneath the Canopy

Beneath the canopy where shadows play,
The world feels alive in a magical way.
With laughter and joy cascading free,
We dance in the glow of a moonlit spree.

The night is alive with tales we share,
Entwined in moments floating in air.
With every heartbeat, we find our grace,
In the festival of life, we embrace.

The Whispering Wind's Stories

The wind sings softly through the trees,
Spreading tales on a fragrant breeze.
Laughter dances in the golden light,
Filling hearts with pure delight.

Children play in meadows wide,
Chasing dreams, the world their guide.
Butterflies flutter, colors bright,
In this realm of joy and light.

Golden sunbeams kiss the ground,
In nature's arms, love is found.
Every whisper, every cheer,
A celebration, warm and clear.

As night descends with stars aglow,
We gather close, our spirits flow.
The whispering wind will never cease,
With every story, hearts find peace.

Beneath the Boughs of Time

Under boughs where shadows play,
Life and laughter find their way.
With every rustle of the leaves,
A tapestry of joy we weave.

A feast of colors, vivid and bright,
Nature's canvas, pure delight.
Birds are chirping, songs so sweet,
Where every heartbeat feels complete.

Side by side, we share our dreams,
In laughter's glow, our spirit beams.
Time stands still beneath this sky,
Together, we will soar and fly.

As dusk embraces day's embrace,
We gather 'round in this safe space.
Stories shared, laughter chimes,
We cherish moments, beneath the boughs of time.

Echoes Through the Frost

In quiet woods, the frost will gleam,
Whispers echo, like a dream.
Beneath the snow, the earth does sigh,
As laughter floats like stars on high.

Winding paths through crystal trees,
Joyful hearts ride winter's breeze.
With every step, the world ignites,
In every corner, festive sights.

The night is sparked with twinkling lights,
While frosty air and warmth ignites.
Underneath a moonlit glow,
We celebrate the magic's flow.

As echoes dance through chilled night air,
We find joy in the moments we share.
With every heartbeat, hearts will toast,
To the echoes of life we cherish most.

A Dance of Shadows and Light

In the twilight where shadows sway,
The world transforms, come out to play.
Candles flicker, stories unfold,
Magic spins in hues of gold.

Laughter rings, a joyous sound,
As friendships bloom, our hearts unbound.
A dance begins beneath the moon,
Together we rise, a festive tune.

With every step, we chase our fears,
In celebration, wipe away tears.
Moments glisten, a vibrant sight,
A tapestry woven with pure delight.

In shadows' arms, we find our spark,
Creating memories in the dark.
A dance of shadows, light takes flight,
Forever swirling in festive night.

Burdens of Boughs Heavy with Snow

The branches bow with gleaming white,
A winter's cloak, a sheer delight.
Children laugh, they build and play,
In this wonderland, joy holds sway.

Candles flicker, warmth inside,
Families gather, hearts open wide.
Songs of cheer fill the chilly air,
Together we weave love everywhere.

Snowflakes dance in the golden light,
Each one unique, a pure delight.
Underneath the frosty sky,
Magic stirs with every sigh.

Evening glows with laughter and cheer,
Echoes of joy we hold so dear.
As burdens lift, and spirits glow,
We cherish these moments in the snow.

Frostbitten Conversations in the Glade

In the quiet woods, whispers near,
Frostbitten words we hold so dear.
The crunch of snow beneath our feet,
Nature's heart, a rhythmic beat.

The trees wear coats of sparkling white,
As we share dreams in soft twilight.
Laughter dances like fireflies,
In this enchanted land, love never dies.

Under the stars, we make a wish,
For moments like these, oh how we relish.
The glade's embrace, a warm cocoon,
Frostbitten whispers beneath the moon.

With every word, the chill subsides,
In joyful echoes, love abides.
Together we weave this magic thread,
In a world of memories, forever spread.

The Last Leaf Falls in Silence

One last leaf clings to its branch,
In the quiet, a fleeting chance.
With a sigh, it dances down,
Covering the earth like a golden gown.

Whispers of autumn in the breeze,
The winds hum soft, they aim to please.
Gathered friends under the trees,
Share joyful stories, hearts at ease.

Every leaf tells tales of old,
Of vibrant hues, of memories bold.
With each fall, a promise made,
Of cycles turning, never to fade.

In this moment, we pause, we breathe,
As nature spins her golden wreath.
For every end, there's a chance to start,
The last leaf falls, yet fills the heart.

Hibernation of Solitude

In quiet slumber, the world slows down,
Wrapped in white like a gentle crown.
Nature rests with a tranquil grace,
Each frosty breath a sacred space.

Inside our homes, warmth beams bright,
As shadows dance in the soft twilight.
We gather close, our hearts entwined,
In the hibernation, we often find.

Stories shared by candlelight,
As winter's chill fades from our sight.
Amidst solitude, joy takes flight,
In the heart's embrace, everything feels right.

Through the stillness, love's light glows,
A festive spirit in all it shows.
In hibernation, we find our song,
A celebration where we all belong.

Winter's Lullaby in the Thorns

Snowflakes dance, in twilight's glow,
The thorns wear white, a gentle show.
Laughter rings, in the chilly air,
Hearts are warm, in winter's care.

Candles flicker, in windows bright,
Stories weave through the cozy night.
Mittens hug, around the mugs,
Joy spills forth, like winter hugs.

Children's voices, a choir of cheer,
Echo through the frosty sphere.
With each breath, a cloud of dream,
Winter's lullaby, a soft theme.

In the thorns, a beauty rare,
Holidays bloom with love to share.
Magic twinkles, in every glance,
Under stars, we laugh and dance.

Beneath the Icicle Sky

Underneath the icicle sky,
Sparkling dreams begin to fly.
Twinkling lights on the crisp white ground,
In this wonder, joy is found.

Chill in the air, but hearts beat warm,
Wrapped in love, away from harm.
Snowmen stand with cheerful grins,
Each day a chance for new begins.

Children sled on hills so steep,
Laughter echoes, memories to keep.
In the hush of a winter night,
Magic glistens, pure delight.

Beneath the stars, we hold each other,
In this season, we find a mother.
With every hug, the warmth we share,
Beneath the sky, we breathe the air.

The Sigh of the Silent Glade

In the glade where whispers dwell,
Nature sings, a gentle spell.
Frosted boughs, a silver sheen,
Eternal calm, a tranquil scene.

Stars cluster in the velvet night,
Every breath feels pure and bright.
Softly falling, snowflakes lie,
In the silence, we hear a sigh.

The world wrapped in a crystal cloak,
Each moment cherished, love awoke.
Together we tread through snowy streams,
In this glade, we weave our dreams.

With every gaze, the wonder's shown,
In winter's heart, we've found our home.
The sigh of beauty lingers near,
In the silent spaces, love draws near.

Frosted Feet on the Path

Frosted feet upon the trail,
Each step whispers a winter tale.
With every crunch, the path we make,
In cold embrace, our spirits wake.

Branches sway with frosty grace,
Nature's wonders, a warm embrace.
The horizon glows, with promise bright,
In winter's arms, we find our light.

Children spinning in joyous delight,
As snowflakes twirl in morning light.
Together we laugh, our worries fade,
In this frosted world, memories laid.

So with each step, we leave our cheer,
In a land where magic's near.
Frosted feet on paths we roam,
With every heartbeat, we find home.

Veils of Mist and Memory

Veils of mist gently sway,
As laughter dances in the air,
Echoes of joy fade away,
Resplendent tales, we all share.

Twinkling lights in the trees,
Adorn the path where we roam,
Soft whispers carried by the breeze,
Hearts entwined, we feel at home.

Beneath the stars, we sing,
Melodies sweet, so divine,
In unity, our voices ring,
In this moment, you are mine.

Celebrate the fleeting night,
With every wish, we ignite,
Memories wrapped in pure delight,
Veils of mist lift with the light.

Emptiness Beneath the Twilight Canopy

A twilight hush blankets the land,
Where shadows stretch and softly creep,
We gather close, hand in hand,
In this silence, our secrets keep.

The sky painted in hues of gold,
Whispers of dreams flutter by,
Each story woven, gently told,
As starlight twinkles in the sky.

Beneath the canopy, we sway,
With laughter brightening the dark,
In shared embrace, we will stay,
While the world ignites a spark.

Emptiness fades into cheer,
As twilight gives way to night,
Together, we'll conquer our fear,
In this festive, radiant light.

Threnody for the Dying Light

The sun sinks low, bids adieu,
Colors blend in a soft embrace,
We gather round to bid it true,
In the twilight, we find our place.

A threnody soft in the air,
Voices lift, a tender song,
With hearts exposed, we strip bare,
In this moment, we all belong.

The last rays kiss the golden grass,
As laughter swirls like fading mist,
Each memory, a glimmering glass,
In the twilight glow, love is kissed.

Though light may fade, yet we sing,
In the shadows, hope shines bright,
Together our hearts take wing,
In threnody for the dying light.

Crystalline Dreams Among the Roots

In the forest where echoes play,
Crystalline dreams spark and ignite,
Beneath the roots, we find our way,
As whispers weave through the night.

Each leaf reflects a shimmering soul,
Unity dances in every gleam,
Nature holds us, makes us whole,
Guided by the moon's soft beam.

In shadows deep, laughter blooms,
Memories rise like gentle streams,
Embraced by the earth's warm womb,
With joy, we cradle our dreams.

Together we'll meld with the threes,
In this festive woodland delight,
Among the roots, we dance with ease,
Crystalline dreams take off in flight.

Lost in the Glistening Pines

Twinkling lights through branches sway,
Joyful whispers in the frosty air.
Laughter dances, night turns to day,
Dreams unfold without a care.

Snowflakes sprinkle on velvet ground,
Glittering paths lead us to bliss.
Nature's beauty, a treasure found,
Moments shared, we shan't miss.

Warmth of friendship, hearts aglow,
Songs of the season fill the night.
Glistening pines, a dazzling show,
In their embrace, we find delight.

As the stars twinkle overhead,
Hope and joy in each gentle breeze.
Under this canopy, worries shed,
In festive spirit, we find ease.

The Hush of the Subzero Woods

In the stillness of a silver night,
Snowflakes twirl, a magical dance.
Frozen whispers bring pure delight,
In the woods, hearts sing and prance.

Chill of winter wraps us tight,
Candles flicker with a soft glow.
Nature sleeps, cloaked in white,
Yet we gather, warmth in tow.

Through the branches, moonbeams peek,
Every shadow, a story to share.
Together we echo, cheek to cheek,
In this festive hush, we declare.

Laughter mingles with the night air,
Hopes and dreams tucked in the snow.
In the subzero, love lays bare,
As we cherish all we know.

Mirror of Ice in the Clearing

Reflecting light, the ice so pure,
A festive realm, each gaze entranced.
In the clearing, joy's allure,
Under the spell of winter's dance.

Footprints trace where memories lie,
Laughter echoes, moments shared.
Under the dome of the starlit sky,
With a warm heart, no soul impaired.

Candles brighten the frozen ground,
With every spark, our spirits lift.
In this mirror, our love is found,
Gifts of joy, the greatest gift.

As we whisper our hopes aloud,
The ice holds secrets, sweet and deep.
Together, we stand hand in hand,
Memories gathered, treasures we keep.

Beneath the Whispering Canopy

Beneath the trees, our laughter flows,
Stars like diamonds in the night.
Joyful hearts, where friendship grows,
In this haven, spirits take flight.

Fireflies dance, a soft-lit glow,
Every moment, a joy to hold.
Nature hums, a gentle flow,
Stories shared, together bold.

In the canopy, we find our peace,
With each whisper, love's refrain.
The festive spirit will never cease,
As we bask in joy's sweet gain.

So here we gather, side by side,
In the comfort of nature's embrace.
Through laughter, tears, and joyful pride,
Together we shine, a warm grace.

Whispers in the Frost

In the glimmer of morning light,
Children laugh in joyful flight.
Footprints mark a dance of cheer,
As winter whispers, drawing near.

Sparkling snowflakes gently fall,
Adorning roofs and windows tall.
Hot cocoa brews with warmth so sweet,
Festive scents around us meet.

Strings of lights in colors bright,
Twinkle softly through the night.
Mirthful songs fill up the air,
Love's embrace is everywhere.

Gathered close where stories weave,
In each glance, we dare believe.
Frosty kisses on our cheeks,
In this moment, joy peaks.

Shadows Among the Pines

Underneath the pines we play,
Chasing twilight into fray.
Laughter echoes through the dark,
Fireflies dance, a glimmering spark.

Bonfires crackle, warmth surrounds,
Music swells with vibrant sounds.
Friends and family close at hand,
Together here, a joyful band.

S'mores and stories shared by light,
The moon above shines crisp and bright.
In the shadows, hearts entwined,
Festive magic softly aligned.

As night deepens, wishes soar,
Dreams take flight, forevermore.
In this haven, bliss we find,
Shadows dance, and life feels kind.

Cold Embrace of Evergreens

Evergreen trees standing tall,
Whispers of nature's wondrous call.
Boughs adorned in frosty lace,
In their arms, we find our place.

Candles flicker, soft and warm,
Gather 'round to share the charm.
Songs of old ring out, so clear,
Spreading warmth and festive cheer.

Snowmen stand with smiles so wide,
Children play, their hearts their guide.
Every moment filled with grace,
In the cold embrace, we trace.

Gifts exchanged with loving care,
Joyous laughter fills the air.
With each hug, the world feels bright,
In this season, pure delight.

Silence Beneath the Canopy

Beneath the canopy we sit,
Nature's wonders gently knit.
Leaves of gold whispering tales,
As laughter rides on gentle gales.

Colors burst, a vibrant show,
Every heart reclaims the glow.
In the forest, friendships bloom,
Dispelling shadows, chasing gloom.

A tapestry of stars above,
Guiding us with endless love.
Quiet moments, joy we find,
Festive warmth, hearts intertwined.

With each breath, the magic grows,
In this silence, bliss bestows.
Gathered close, we share our dreams,
Underneath the moonlight beams.

The Stillness of Winter's Heart

In the hush, the snowflakes dance,
Whispers weave in icy trance.
Lights twinkle on branches bare,
Joyful laughter fills the air.

Fires crackle, warmth abounds,
Hope and cheer in joyful sounds.
Families gather, tales unfold,
Magic glimmers, bright and bold.

Gifts wrapped tight with ribbons gleam,
Soft carols sing like a dream.
Frozen beauty all around,
In this stillness, love is found.

Stars above, a twinkling show,
Hearts ignite with winter's glow.
In each breath, the season's cheer,
Winter's heart, so bright and near.

Rime Collected on Mossy Stones

Morning breaks with a silver sheen,
Mossy stones, where few have been.
Frosty crystals catch the light,
Nature's jewels, pure delight.

The brook sings softly, clear and bright,
Murmurs echo with pure delight.
Each leaf shimmers, brushed with frost,
In this moment, nothing's lost.

Gathered whispers of the dawn,
In every breath, life is drawn.
A tapestry of chill and cheer,
Rime collected, winter's spear.

Together with the fading night,
Frost enthralls with its chilly bite.
Nature's artwork, pure and true,
Rime and moss, stitched in blue.

Drifting Secrets in the Pale Moonlight

Beneath the pale, enchanting glow,
Whispers of the night do flow.
Dreams unfurl in shadows cast,
Secrets shared, too sweet to last.

Stars above, a shining sea,
Tales of magic, wild and free.
Moonlit paths where lovers tread,
Softly spoken words are said.

In the twilight, shadows play,
Dancing whispers drift away.
Every heartbeat, every sigh,
Drifting secrets, soaring high.

Holding close the night's embrace,
Finding peace in time and space.
In this moment, worlds unite,
Lost in dreams, 'neath moonlit light.

A Tapestry of Twisted Branches

In a grove where shadows weave,
Twisted branches dance and cleave.
Colors splash in autumn's grace,
Nature's beauty, warm embrace.

Leaves fall gently, painting ground,
Rustling whispers, soft and round.
The air, alight with crisp delight,
Festive spirits take their flight.

Birds create a symphony,
Calling forth the mystery.
In the twilight, laughter sings,
Celebration, life it brings.

Gathered friends and joyous hearts,
Together, never far apart.
In this grove, the magic stays,
A tapestry of joyful days.

Sighs of the Ancient Forest

In canopies where whispers dwell,
Golden light begins to swell.
Joyful birds in chorus sing,
The magic of the forest spring.

Leaves like laughter dance with glee,
Such wonder in each swaying tree.
Mossy carpets, soft and bright,
Guide our hearts to pure delight.

Sunbeams trickle down the trunks,
Amid the lively, cheerful clunks.
Nature's symphony, a sweet embrace,
Filling every sacred space.

Here, where every shadow plays,
We celebrate the golden days.
In the ancient woods we roam,
Finding joy in nature's home.

Nature's Frosted Reverie

Snowflakes twirl in frosty air,
Whispers of winter everywhere.
Sparkling gems on branches cling,
Nature's canvas in the spring.

Children laugh, their cheeks aglow,
Building dreams in winter's show.
Hot cocoa warms in chilly hands,
Together conquering snowy lands.

Frosted fields in morning light,
Glittering like stars at night.
Nature's breath, a chilly tune,
Dances under the light of the moon.

With every step, a joyful cheer,
Creating memories, season dear.
In this frosted world we find,
Nature's magic intertwined.

Shivers Within the Thicket

In gentle breezes, secrets play,
Among the shadows where we stray.
A rustle here, a fleeting sight,
The thicket holds its festive light.

Crickets chirp, a rhythmic beat,
As fireflies dance on tiny feet.
Nature's party, wild and free,
We celebrate this jubilee.

Leaves like confetti fill the air,
Whispers of joy everywhere.
Mirthful laughter, echoes clear,
In this thicket, hearts draw near.

Stars peek out, in velvet skies,
Welcoming dreams, where magic lies.
With open hearts, we come alive,
In the thicket, together we thrive.

A Serenade in the Quietude

Beneath the boughs of whispering trees,
Nature sings upon the breeze.
A chorus soft, serene, and bright,
Guiding our souls into the night.

Crickets strum their evening song,
With every note, where we belong.
Moonlight dances on the stream,
Awakening our sweetest dream.

Stars above join in the cheer,
Illuminating paths so near.
In quietude, our hearts embrace,
Finding joy in peaceful grace.

Each heartbeat sings of love anew,
In nature's arms, the world feels true.
As night unfolds her velvet hue,
Together, let us start anew.

Secrets of the Starlit Canopy

Beneath the stars, we gather near,
Whispers of magic, laughter clear.
Dancing shadows, twinkling bright,
Secrets hidden in the night.

Moonbeams waltz on velvet ground,
Hearts aflutter, joy unbound.
Close your eyes and feel the thrill,
Wonders waiting, time stands still.

Fireflies flicker, casting dreams,
In this moment, nothing seems
Out of reach; our spirits soar,
Together, we will find much more.

With every glance, stories unfold,
Tales of love, both brave and bold.
Underneath this starlit glow,
We weave a tapestry of flow.

Crisp Air and Echoed Footsteps

Crisp air whispers through the trees,
Echoed footsteps, carried breeze.
Golden leaves beneath our feet,
Nature's rhythm, heartbeats sweet.

Laughter dances in the chill,
Moments cherished, time stands still.
Together we roam, hand in hand,
Mapping dreams across the land.

Hot cocoa warming every soul,
Stories shared, a perfect goal.
Under the arch of twilight's hue,
Friendship blooms, forever true.

Darkening skies, stars emerge bright,
Our spirits shine in the night.
With every step, a journey made,
In this bliss, we are not afraid.

Fable of the Forgotten Trail

Through the woods, we wander free,
A fable waits, a history.
Whispers echo from days of old,
Tales of magic yet untold.

Amongst the trees, a secret glows,
In every breeze, the ancient flows.
Paths that twist and turn anew,
Invite the brave, inspire the few.

With each step, the past awakes,
Echoing laughter, playful stakes.
Gather close, the fire ignites,
Fables shared on starry nights.

Together, we embrace the lore,
Crafting dreams, forevermore.
On this trail, our spirits blend,
As the fable has no end.

Frostbitten Tales of Yore

In the frost, the stories gleam,
Tales of magic, hope, and dream.
Winter's breath on cheeks so warm,
Keeps our hearts in perfect form.

Candles flicker, casting glow,
Frostbitten branches dance below.
Gather 'round, let laughter ring,
In our hearts, the joy we bring.

Snowflakes whisper of times long past,
Moments frozen, memories cast.
Each tale spun in gentle snow,
Invites us closer, hearts aglow.

Beneath the stars, our voices blend,
Frostbitten tales that never end.
In this season, bonds we forge,
A celebration we all gorge.

Echoes Through Gnarled Branches

Laughter dances in the air,
Joyful whispers everywhere.
Underneath the moonlit sky,
We celebrate, our hearts so high.

Colors twinkle, spirits soar,
Each moment cherished, we explore.
With friends gathered, the night aglow,
In this magic, our love will grow.

Songs of old enchant the breeze,
Spinning tales beneath the trees.
Echoes linger, sweet and clear,
Creating bonds we hold so dear.

As gnarled branches sway and sway,
We find our peace in this display.
With hearts open wide, we embrace,
Joyful memories time can't erase.

Mist and Mirth in the Thicket

A soft mist hugs the mossy ground,
In the thicket, laughter is found.
Mirthful spirits dart and play,
Chasing shadows, bright as day.

With each step, the flowers bloom,
Embracing spring in joyful plume.
Voices echo through the leaves,
Filling hearts like webs that weave.

Candles flicker, stories shared,
In this moment, we are paired.
Smiles and memories intertwine,
In the thicket, all is divine.

Mist and mirth create a glow,
As time pauses, soft and slow.
Families gather, friends unite,
In the thicket, pure delight.

A Shroud of Silver Air

Silver air wraps the world so tight,
Stars awaken in the heart of night.
Voices blend in harmony near,
Songs and laughter fill the sphere.

Beneath the sky, we raise our cheer,
Celebrating all we hold dear.
Dancing shadows, dreams take flight,
In this moment, all feels right.

The sparkle of joy lights our way,
As memories spark and softly sway.
In a shroud of silver bliss,
We find comfort in each kiss.

Together we stand, hand in hand,
Creating magic, oh so grand.
In this night, forever we'll stay,
Wrapped in love till break of day.

The Stillness Between the Trees

In the stillness, time stands still,
Joyful whispers move at will.
Between the trees, laughter springs,
A festive air that nature brings.

Gentle breezes softly play,
Carrying our smiles away.
Underneath the stars above,
We gather here, united in love.

Flickering lights, a glowing hue,
Hearts entwined, just me and you.
Together we dance, spirits rise,
Echoes of laughter pierce the skies.

The stillness holds a sacred space,
Each memory etched, a warm embrace.
In this moment, we all belong,
As nature hums its soft, sweet song.

Inked Stories of Winter's Night

Moonlight dances on the snow,
Whispers of joy begin to flow.
Fires crackle, laughter rings bright,
Inked stories unfold this night.

Footprints trace tales of delight,
Children's giggles, pure and light.
Blankets wrapped, warm in embrace,
Hearts aglow in this cherished place.

Stars twinkle with a festive cheer,
Gathered friends, all those held dear.
Toasts are made, memories shared,
In the warmth of love declared.

As snowflakes fall, dreams take flight,
Inked stories grace this winter's night.
Hope and joy weave through the air,
A celebration beyond compare.

Underneath the Stars

Beneath the sky where dreams ignite,
The world is bathed in shimmering light.
Friends embrace in twilight's glow,
A symphony of laughter flows.

Candles flicker, shadows dance,
Each moment filled with sweet romance.
Joy cascades like floral blooms,
Love's warm embrace through starry rooms.

Sipping warm cider, hearts entwine,
Stories woven through the vine.
Beneath the stars, bright and free,
Together is where we long to be.

As night unfolds its velvet shawl,
Underneath these stars, we stand tall.
With whispers soft, our dreams take flight,
In this festive, magical night.

The World Pauses

In the hush of a snowy day,
The world pauses, comes out to play.
Joyous spirits rise and sing,
Celebrating this wondrous thing.

Glittering snowflakes softly fall,
Gather around, we heed the call.
Laughter echoes through the trees,
Caught in the warm, gentle breeze.

Fires glow with a soothing light,
As night wraps us, snug and tight.
With stories told and hearts so bold,
The world pauses, joy unfolds.

In moments shared, we find our bliss,
Each festive thought sealed with a kiss.
For in stillness, love exemplifies,
As the world pauses, laughter flies.

The Lace of Dawn on Sleepy Branches

The lace of dawn, so soft and sweet,
Coats the branches, a delicate sheet.
Whispers of morning fill the air,
A festive promise lingers there.

Golden rays break through the trees,
Awakening joys on a gentle breeze.
Birds sing songs, a fresh new start,
Edging closer to every heart.

The world adorned in hues so bright,
Sparkling like diamonds in morning light.
In every nook, a story to tell,
As sleepy branches bid fare-thee-well.

With each new dawn, life intertwines,
Festivity in nature's designs.
A vibrant tapestry, hope imbibes,
The lace of dawn as joy describes.

Remnants of Color Amidst Grays

A canvas stretched, where grays embrace,
Remnants of color dance with grace.
In winter's chill, bright blooms arise,
Festive hues greet our eager eyes.

Scarves wrapped tight, we venture out,
In splashes of color, we laugh and shout.
A holiday spirit fills the air,
As vibrant hearts let go of care.

Pine cones glisten, berries bright red,
Nature's palette, where joy is spread.
From gray to gold, our spirits soar,
In winter's embrace, we ask for more.

Remnants of color paint the scene,
A reminder of hope, a tranquil dream.
Together we gather, joy aligns,
Amidst the grays, our love shines.

Stillness Inside the Forest's Heart

In the grove where shadows play,
Whispers dance among the leaves,
Nature's laughter in the sway,
Joyful tune the forest weaves.

Sunlight glimmers, soft and warm,
Burbling streams with secrets sing,
Branches twirl, the trunks transform,
Festive spirits take to wing.

Crimson blooms in colors bright,
Petals sway like gentle dreams,
In the calm of golden light,
Every silence softly gleams.

As the evening paints the sky,
Stars awake on velvet seas,
In the choir of night birds' cry,
Nature hums her joyous peace.

A Time When the Earth Holds Its Breath

When spring unfurls her vibrant lace,
The world pauses, wrapped in cheer,
Colors burst with gentle grace,
Magic whispers, spring draws near.

Petals dance on zephyr's wing,
Laughter ripples through the air,
Joyous songs the robins sing,
In the hush, we find our prayer.

Underneath the blossomed trees,
Nature's pulse, a sacred beat,
In the garden's gentle breeze,
Life awakens, bittersweet.

In this moment, hearts unite,
Gathered round in sweet delight,
Every breath a blissful hymn,
In the stillness, dreams grow dim.

Lurking Spirits of the Ancient Trees

Shadows stretch in twilight's glow,
Ancient spirits swirl and twine,
In the silence, tales unfold,
Nature's magic, pure, divine.

Echoes of a time long past,
Whispers brush against my ear,
In the boughs, their secrets cast,
Lurking softly, ever near.

Branches sway with gentle ease,
Dancing in the moonlight's beam,
Harvests of the past release,
Silent prayers in twilight's dream.

Owl calls out a haunting song,
Night reveals a canvas bright,
In this forest, I belong,
Lost within the starry night.

Ghosts of Autumn in Frozen Slumber

Leaves like laughter drift and twirl,
Crisp air dancing on the tongue,
As the chill begins to swirl,
Autumn's song is softly sung.

Ghosts of summer whisper low,
Echoing through twilight's haze,
Colors blaze as breezes blow,
In the twilight, sunlight plays.

Frosted mornings, gleaming bright,
Nature cloaked in silver grace,
Embers glow in fading light,
Time stands still, a warm embrace.

As the world begins to sleep,
Dreams of harvest fill the air,
In this stillness, memories creep,
Memories crafted with care.

The Haunting Silence of Nightfall

As stars peek out, the day must rest,
The moon reveals her silver crest.
Whispers dance through the cool night air,
With dreams unfolding everywhere.

Laughter echoes in the twilight glow,
In shadows where gentle breezes flow.
A festive spirit begins to rise,
As joy ignites under starlit skies.

Shadows That Linger After Dark

Underneath the twilight's embrace,
Shadows twirl with a lively pace.
Festive hearts in a merry trance,
Even the stars seem keen to dance.

Whirls of laughter fill the cool night,
In every corner, a flickering light.
The air is alive with jubilant cheer,
As the essence of festivity draws near.

Fragments of Light in the Dusk

With colors bursting across the sky,
The day bids farewell, we wave goodbye.
Fragments of light, a playful sight,
Spark the spirit of a joyful night.

Crisp autumn leaves in a swirling dance,
Invite all to join in their enchanting chance.
As candles flicker and laughter ignites,
The dusk transforms into wonderful nights.

Tales Told by the Howling Wind

Listen closely to the stories spun,
By the howling wind, a playful fun.
Each whisper wraps the world in delight,
Bringing the festive chill of the night.

With every gust, old legends revive,
In the tapestry of night, we thrive.
A celebration sung in nature's round,
As the earth spins with joy, a sweet sound.

Veil of the Frozen Boughs

In whispers light, the snowflakes fall,
A frosty dance, a winter's ball.
Boughs draped in white, like lace they glow,
Under the stars, where the cold winds blow.

Laughter rings in the crisp, clear night,
Children play in the soft moonlight.
Joyful melodies fill the air,
As warmth and cheer replace all care.

Candles flicker in windows bright,
Sharing warmth in the deep of night.
Voices lift in a festive cheer,
For love and joy are gathered near.

With every breath, the magic grows,
Wrapped in the hush of falling snows.
Together we weave a tale untold,
In the frozen boughs, our hearts unfold.

Lament of the Sleepy Hollow

In quiet woods where shadows creep,
The Hollow sings, but not of sleep.
A gentle breeze through branches sighs,
As ancient tales of joy arise.

Around the fire, stories weave,
Of whispered love, and hearts that cleave.
Though ghostly shades in moonlight roam,
They chase our fears, and lead us home.

With each crackle of the flame's tease,
The air is sweet with memories.
We dance in light, as shadows blend,
And find our hearts begin to mend.

So raise your glass to nights like this,
To laughter's warmth and moments kissed.
For in the dark, the bright stars gleam,
And every heart can find its dream.

Secrets in the Pine Needles

Beneath the pines where secrets lie,
The whispers dance, they soar and fly.
A gentle rustle in the air,
Invites us all to dream and share.

With every step on needle's ground,
A magic pulse, a hidden sound.
The forest hums a festive tune,
As hearts uplift beneath the moon.

From every branch, a sparkle glows,
As laughter echoes where love flows.
Together we tread this snow-kissed trail,
Where ancient secrets sweetly sail.

Let's gather 'round the fire's embrace,
In this warm, enchanted place.
For in the pines, we find our way,
And cherish life on this bright day.

Frost on the Bark

The trees stand tall, adorned with grace,
In twilight's glow, a frosty lace.
Whispers of winter in the air,
As nature's gifts are laid with care.

Frost on the bark, a shimmering sight,
Reflecting dreams in the pale moonlight.
Each twinkle speaks of tales to tell,
Of laughter, hope, and joy to dwell.

So gather near, let spirits rise,
In the cozy warmth where friendship lies.
With every heartbeat, joy expands,
As winter's magic nears our hands.

The world is bright, let shadows flee,
With festive hearts, we shall be free.
In frosted whispers and bright delight,
Together we shine in the starry night.

Shadows on the Woodland Trail

Beneath the canopies, laughter rings,
As children dance and the melodies sing.
Fruits of the forest, so bright and sweet,
The festive spirit, a joyful treat.

With lanterns aglow, the night draws near,
Whispers of joy in the air we hear.
Footprints across the soft, leafy ground,
In shadows, the magic of joy is found.

Gathered around the flickering flame,
Every face knows the other's name.
Stories and songs lift our hearts so high,
Under the starlit, twinkling sky.

The woodland alive with our laughter's call,
In unison we'd rise, together we'd fall.
Nature's embrace, a warm, soft light,
With shadows of joy, we dance through the night.

Whispers of the Frostbitten Hollow

In frost-kissed woods, where the whispers blend,
Festivity blooms, as seasons transcend.
Crystal branches sparkle, dressed in white,
Echoes of laughter twirl in the night.

Hearts stitched together, warm 'round the fire,
Stories shared softly, lifting us higher.
The chill in the air, a thrilling delight,
As friends gather 'round and the stars shine bright.

Frost blooms like flowers, twinkling so clear,
With each breath we take, winter's magic appears.
The hollow a canvas of wonders untold,
Where tales of the past now shimmering gold.

United in joy, we revel and cheer,
Each glimmering moment, forever so dear.
With snowflakes a-fall, our spirits take flight,
In whispers of warmth on a frosty night.

The Whispering Trees of Winter

Beneath the frost, with secrets untold,
The trees stand watchful, so regal, so bold.
In whispers of winter, they chime and sway,
Carrying tales from the bright summer day.

With each gentle gust, the laughter escapes,
Echoes of joy in the curious shapes.
As branches entwine, in festive embrace,
A symphony plays, a warm, timeless grace.

Candles alight on the snowy terrain,
Mirth and enchantment flow free like the rain.
Together we gather, our voices in song,
Under the trees where we all belong.

The chill in the air cannot dampen our cheer,
For the whispering trees hold our loved ones near.
In this winter wonderland, perfectly spun,
Each moment a treasure, each heart full of fun.

A Breath of Frigid Air

A breath of frigid air fills the night,
Wrapped in warmth, our hearts feel so light.
Every twinkling star overhead, a cheer,
In this festival season, love draws us near.

Snowflakes are dancers, spinning in grace,
Painting a canvas, this magical space.
From bundled up whispers to joyous delight,
We gather together beneath the soft light.

With mugs full of cocoa and smiles so wide,
In the glow of the hearth, we take in the ride.
As laughter and music drift through the air,
Each moment we capture, a memory to share.

Through the chill of the night, our spirits ignite,
In a world shimmering brightly, everything feels right.
As a breath of winter whispers good cheer,
Each heartbeat entwined, so festive, so clear.

Solstice Reflections in the Woods

In the depths of the pines, we gather bright,
With laughter that dances like firelight.
The shadows grow long, wrapping us tight,
In the joy of the night, all feels just right.

Stars sprinkle the sky like confetti fair,
Whispers of magic flow through the air.
Warmth in our hearts, and love we can share,
Each moment infused with a festive flare.

Flickering lights on the branches sway,
As memories twirl in a luminous play.
With friends by our side, we cherish today,
In this solstice glow, let our spirits stay.

Candles aglow, we toast to the end,
Of seasons that change, and friendships we tend.
With songs that uplift, our voices blend,
In this woodland fest, may the joy never bend.

The Breath of a Distant Storm

In the distance, the thunder rolls deep,
As clouds gather round, secrets they keep.
The dance of the raindrops begins to creep,
While we hold on tight, our joys we will reap.

The air is electric, charged with the thrill,
A festival of nature, a wondrous chill.
As branches sway gently, we savor the thrill,
United in laughter, our hearts fill to spill.

A sudden downpour, a curtain of grace,
We run to the shelter, find warmth in this place.
With cheer in our hearts and smiles on each face,
In the breath of the storm, we embrace this space.

Then the sky starts to clear, a canvas so bright,
With raindrops still glistening, catching the light.
In every fresh breath, there's a sense of delight,
As the world celebrates the magic in sight.

Gnarled Roots and Cold Embraces

Beneath arching boughs, where shadows play warm,
We wander through pathways, a natural charm.
Leaves rustle softly, a comforting harm,
In the gnarled roots' hold, we weather the storm.

The chill in the air dances close to our cheeks,
With fireside tales, it's connection we seek.
In the heart of the forest, our spirits speak,
In the cold embraces, our bonds won't feel weak.

Stars twinkle above in welcoming arcs,
As laughter rings out, igniting the sparks.
Each story we share leaves indelible marks,
With gnarled roots grounding our way like larks.

Together we stand, as nightfall descends,
With warmth in our hearts, the joy never ends.
In the embrace of the woods, as nature blends,
We find solace and light, through shadows our friends.

A Palette of Grays in Twilight

In twilight's soft glow, the colors may fade,
But the beauty in gray, it simply won't trade.
A canvas of shadows, where dreams are made,
We gather in stillness, our worries delayed.

The whispers of dusk wrap around in a hush,
A symphony played in the evening's soft blush.
In the palette of life, we feel the sweet rush,
Of moments together, no anger will crush.

With laughter like lanterns, we light up the night,
In shadows we shine, an enchanting sight.
The palette of grays holds a truth so bright,
In silence we find the warmth of our light.

As the stars gently flicker, painting the skies,
A reminder that joy in simplicity lies.
In a palette of grays, where connection complies,
We celebrate life as the evening replies.